CARRIE UNDERWOOD

by E. Merwin

Consultant: Starshine Roshell
Music and Entertainment Journalist
Santa Barbara, California

BEARPORT
PUBLISHING

New York, New York

Credits

Cover, © Rich Fury/Invision/AP Photo; 4, © Chris Pizzello/Reuters/Newscom; 5, © Chris Pizzello/Reuters/Newscom; 6, Courtesy Seth Poppel Yearbook Library; 7, © Elegeyda/Shutterstock; 8, © Ufukguler/Dreamstime.com; 9, © The Oklahoman; 10, Courtesy Seth Poppel Yearbook Library; 11, © WENN Ltd./Alamy Stock; 12, © Kooslin/Dreamstime; 13, © AP Photo/The Oklahoman/Paul Hellstern; 14, Courtesy SPG; 15, © Mike Blake/Reuters/Newscom; 17, © AP Photo/Michael Zorn/Invision; 18, Courtesy Eva Rinaldi/Wikimedia CC; 19, © Splash News/Alamy Stock; 20, © Sbukley/Dreamstime; 21, © Mario Anzuoni/Reuters/Newscom; 22T, © Chris Pizzello/Reuters/Newscom; 22B, © Evgeney Karandaev/Shutterstock.

Publisher: Kenn Goin
Creative Director: Spencer Brinker
Production and Photo Research: Shoreline Publishing Group LLC

Library of Congress Cataloging-in-Publication Data

Names: Merwin, E. author. | Roshell, Starshine.
Title: Carrie Underwood / by E. Merwin ; consultant: Starshine Roshell.
Description: New York, New York : Bearport Publishing, 2019. | Series:
   Amazing Americans: Country music stars | Includes bibliographical
   references and index.
Identifiers: LCCN 2018011082 (print) | LCCN 2018012371 (ebook) |
   ISBN 9781684027293 (ebook) | ISBN 9781684026838 (library)
Subjects: LCSH: Underwood, Carrie, 1983-–Juvenile literature. | Country
   musicians—United States—Biography—Juvenile literature.
Classification: LCC ML3930.U53 (ebook) | LCC ML3930.U53 M47 2019 (print) |
   DDC 782.421642092 [B] —dc23
LC record available at https://lccn.loc.gov/2018011082

For more information, write to Bearport Publishing Company, Inc., 45 West 21st Street, Suite 3B, New York, New York 10010. Printed in the United States of America.

10 9 8 7 6 5 4 3 2 1

CONTENTS

An American Idol

Wearing a glittering gown, Carrie Underwood stood nervously before the *American Idol* judges. Then they called her name—she had won! Carrie cried with joy. She thanked America and sang "Inside Your Heaven" as fans cheered.

Carrie got a hug from her mother, Carole, after she won *American Idol*.

4

Carrie's victory in 2005 set an *American Idol* record. During that season, more than 500 million votes were sent in by viewers.

5

Country Girl

Carrie Marie Underwood was born on March 10, 1983, in Muskogee, Oklahoma. Carrie grew up on a farm with lots of animals. "I enjoyed things like playing on dirt roads, climbing trees . . . and, of course, singing," Carrie said. She loved country life.

Carrie in third grade

When Carrie grew up and left Oklahoma, she missed her animals. When her dad called, he would put the phone up to the animals' ears. That way, Carrie could speak to them!

7

Hometown Hero

Growing up, Carrie often sang in church. She also performed at special events and talent shows. One neighbor was amazed by her voice. When Carrie was 14, the neighbor got her an **audition** with a record company. The company didn't hire her. Carrie said, "Everything has a way of working out."

Carrie performing at the Oklahoma Music Hall of Fame

Eventually, things really did work out for Carrie. In 2008, she was voted into the Oklahoma Music Hall of Fame. It's in her hometown of Muskogee.

9

Quarterback

In high school, Carrie was a great student. She also loved to perform on stage. She had other talents, too. Carrie played basketball and softball. She was even a **quarterback** on the school's all-girl football team! Carrie recalls, "Not to brag, but I could throw as far as I needed to."

Carrie practices piano at home.

Carrie graduated with honors from her high school in 2001.

Carrie used the softball skills she learned in high school in this 2012 charity game.

Winning Waitress

After high school, Carrie attended Northeastern State University in Oklahoma. She studied **journalism**. To pay for college, she worked at a pizzeria. She had no idea she would soon be famous. When she won *American Idol* in 2005, Carrie received a million-dollar record deal. Still, Carrie attended her college graduation in 2006.

On her graduation day, reporters wanted to talk to Carrie. She refused. She wanted her fellow students to get the same attention that she got.

13

Some Hearts

In 2005, Carrie released her first album, *Some Hearts*. It rocketed to success! It became one of the best-selling **debut** albums in country music history. Worldwide, it sold over eight million copies. The album led to two Grammy Awards in 2007. One of them was for Best New Artist.

Carrie's first album was a huge smash!

All of Carrie's five albums have been hits. In total, she has sold over 65 million albums and won over 160 awards!

Carrie with her first two Grammy Awards

15

Storyteller

In 2015, Carrie released her fifth album, *Storyteller*. Like the others, it went **platinum**. In addition to being a top performer, Carrie is also a talented songwriter. For *Storyteller*, Carrie wrote six songs, including the number-one hit "Heartbeat." On her *Storyteller* tour in 2016, Carrie traveled to Europe and Canada. Over a million people came to see her!

In 2017, Carrie released a film called *The Storyteller Tour: Live from Madison Square Garden.*

Carrie sings at New York City's Madison Square Garden in 2016.

Freefalling

What does a superstar do for fun? While touring in Australia, Carrie decided to try skydiving. At first, she felt nervous. When she jumped, however, she said she felt like a "superhero." After it was over, Carrie tweeted, "I can't believe I did this!"

Carrie performs at the Sydney Opera House during a visit to Australia.

Carrie took her dog Ace with her when she went on tour.

Carrie also enjoys yoga, watching scary movies, and walking her dogs.

Idol Gives Back

Carrie also makes time to help others. In 2008, Carrie added her voice to *Idol Gives Back*. The event raised money for people in need. In her hometown, Carrie started a **foundation** that gives musical instruments and other supplies to schools. She says, "I feel blessed to be able to create something as a way of giving back."

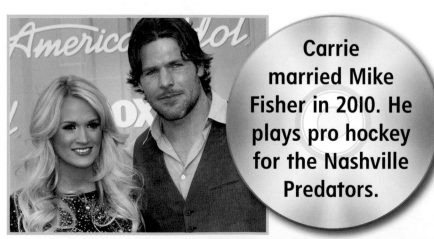

Carrie married Mike Fisher in 2010. He plays pro hockey for the Nashville Predators.

Carries sings at the 2008 *Idol Gives Back* concert in New York City.

Timeline

Here are some key dates in Carrie Underwood's life.

1980 — 1990 — 2000 — 2010 — 2020

March 10, 1983
Carrie Marie Underwood is born in Muskogee, Oklahoma.

2005
Wins first place in the fourth season of *American Idol*

2005
Releases her debut album, *Some Hearts*

2006
Graduates from Northeastern State University

2007
Wins two Grammy Awards, including Best New Artist

2008
Creates a foundation to help schools in her hometown

2015
Releases her fifth album, *Storyteller*

2016
Travels to Europe and Canada on her fifth concert tour

2017
Storyteller tour film is released

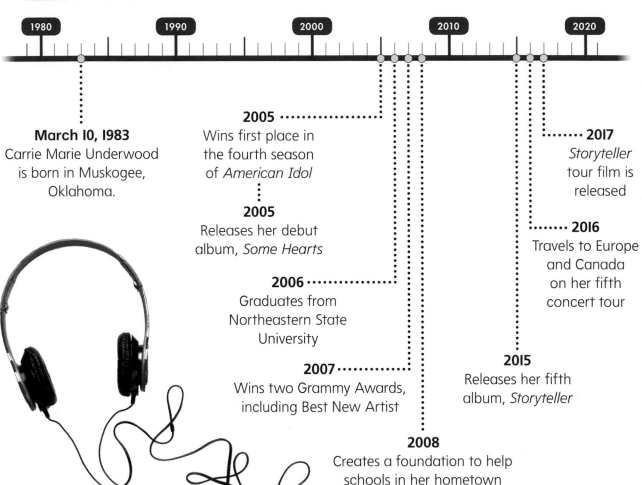

Glossary

audition (aw-DISH-uhn) a short performance by a singer to see whether he or she has skill

debut (day-BYOO) a public appearance for the first time

foundation (foun-DAY-shuhn) an organization that supports or gives money to worthwhile causes

journalism (JUR-nuhl-iz-uhm) the profession of writing or reporting news stories

platinum (PLAT-in-uhm) an award given for albums that sell more than a million copies

quarterback (KWOR-tur-bak) a football player who passes the ball and leads a team to touchdowns

Index

Read More

Brooks, Riley. *Carrie Underwood: American Dream.* New York: Scholastic (2013).

Burns, Kylie. *Carrie Underwood (Superstars!).* New York: Crabtree (2013).

Learn More Online

To learn more about Carrie Underwood, visit
www.bearportpublishing.com/AmazingAmericans

About the Author

E. Merwin enjoys writing about artists who teach us to believe in our talents and follow our dreams.